START SMALL, THINK BIG

small speckled
Egg

START SMALL, THINK BIG

small speckled Egg

by Mary Auld

illustrations by
Anna Terreros-Martin

RED COMET PRESS • BROOKLYN

Here is a small speckled egg.
Here is the bird who laid the egg.
She is an arctic tern.
She is my mother.

ARCTIC
June

Her speckled egg is hard to spot in its grass-lined nest.

She sits on my egg
to keep it warm on
the stony ground.

Inside the egg, I am growing.

If the egg were see-through, you would see the start of new life. This is an embryo that will grow into a baby bird.

Here I am, a small, fluffy, downy chick hatched from my egg. I am ready to be fed.

The chick has pecked and wriggled her way out of her shell.

For three days she is too small to leave the nest. The parents feed her straight away.

The parents find each other by their calls. They say, "Here I am!" in the middle of all the other nesting birds.

Here is our colony of terns.

We all nest together by the cold Arctic Sea.
The sea is full of fish—our favorite food.

Terns form nesting colonies in a place in the far north called the Arctic. They spend the sunny spring and summer here.

*Can you spot the hungry arctic fox?
One parent calls out "Danger!"
and the terns are on guard.*

Look out for dive-bombers, fox!

Living in a colony helps protect the chicks from danger. The adult terns work together to scare off predators.

Even in the cold Arctic, there are predators who prey on eggs and chicks. Predators include polar bears and seagulls, as well as arctic foxes.

The parents dive down at high speed, striking the predator. A tern's beak is sharp! The predator usually runs away.

Here I am, a growing chick.
I'm always hungry and cry for food.
Can you see my feathers peeking
through my fluffy down?

Both my parents feed me. The food gives me the energy I need to live and grow.

Terns skim the water with their beaks or make shallow dives to catch small fish and shellfish.

In the Arctic, the days become very long in the summer. For a few weeks, the sun does not set at all. This gives the terns plenty of time to find food.

Here I am, a young bird with all my feathers.
I flap and stretch my wings. I am ready to fly.

After three to four weeks, the chick is fully fledged. Her feathers are speckled and not as strongly marked as her parents. Her beak and legs are dark.

Her parents teach her to fly.
Of all birds, terns are one of the most expert at flying.

I can glide...

Terns float in the air with their wings spread.

I can hover...

Terns flap their wings very fast to stay in one place like a hawk.

I can dive...

Terns fold their wings to plunge into the water.

And catch my first fish!

Here is my family in the setting sun. The days are getting shorter. It is time to fly south.

Terns migrate. As the seasons change, they fly in search of food.

The Arctic summer is short. By early August, it is stormy and there is less daylight. It makes it difficult for the terns to fish.

A tern colony is a noisy place. It falls silent just before the birds migrate. This silence is called a "dread."

**Here is silence.
The colony is waiting.**

One bird flies up . . .
and we all take off!

**I follow my parents over the Atlantic Ocean.
I am only three months old.**

The terns can sleep on the wing and do not land for days. Far out in the ocean, they fish for food. The food gives them the energy for their onward journey.

The colony splits up.

My family flies where the wind takes us—
to the coast of Africa and beyond.
Sometimes we pause to rest and feed.

Terns make use of the strong winds on their migration. The winds blow some terns to the coast of Africa and some to the coast of South America. They find their way south from there by following the coast.

Here I am resting on an iceberg in Antarctica. I have arrived!

ANTARCTIC
October to February

The terns feed all the long days of the Antarctic summer.

By following the seasons, the terns are able to find fish all year round and avoid the dark of winter and its bad weather.

Then, as the days shorten, my family will head back to the Arctic again.
We take a fast route, swooshing north on the wind.

Here I am, now an adult tern.
I am back in the Arctic.
I will make this journey every year of my life.

The terns return to the same colony in the Arctic every year. They may live for over 30 years.

Here is the nest we have made together.
In it, I have laid a small speckled egg.

open

START SMALL...

This is the life cycle that begins with a small speckled egg and leads to a beautiful adult tern. An arctic tern can live for 30 years.

Terns do not just use their eyes to find their way. They feel the Earth's magnetism, an invisible force field that surrounds the Earth. It is strongest at the Arctic and the Antarctic.

THINK BIG!

MORE DAYLIGHT HOURS
Migrating from pole to pole, arctic terns follow the long daylight hours of summer at either end of the Earth. This gives them more daylight hours than any other animal on our planet.

THE LONGEST MIGRATION
Every year, a tern will fly over 44,000 miles between the Arctic and Antarctic. It's the longest migration of any animal on the Earth.

AMAZING NAVIGATION SKILLS
Terns return to the same place in the Arctic each year to nest in the same colony. To do this, they follow coastlines and use the pull of the invisible magnetic force field around the Earth.

TO THE MOON AND BACK
In their lifetimes, arctic terns may fly up to 1.5 million miles. That's the same as flying from the Earth to the Moon and back again over three times.

FLYING NORTH
March to April

OTHER TITLES

  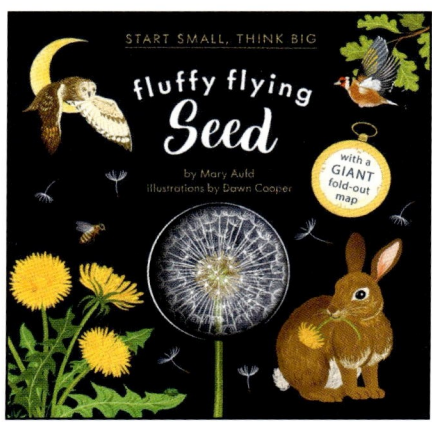

COMING SOON

SMALL SPARKLING RAINDROP

SMALL MIGHTY BEETLE

StartSmallThinkBigBooks.com

Terns usually mate for life. They hatch and raise between one and three chicks each year. That's around 50 chicks in their lifetime.

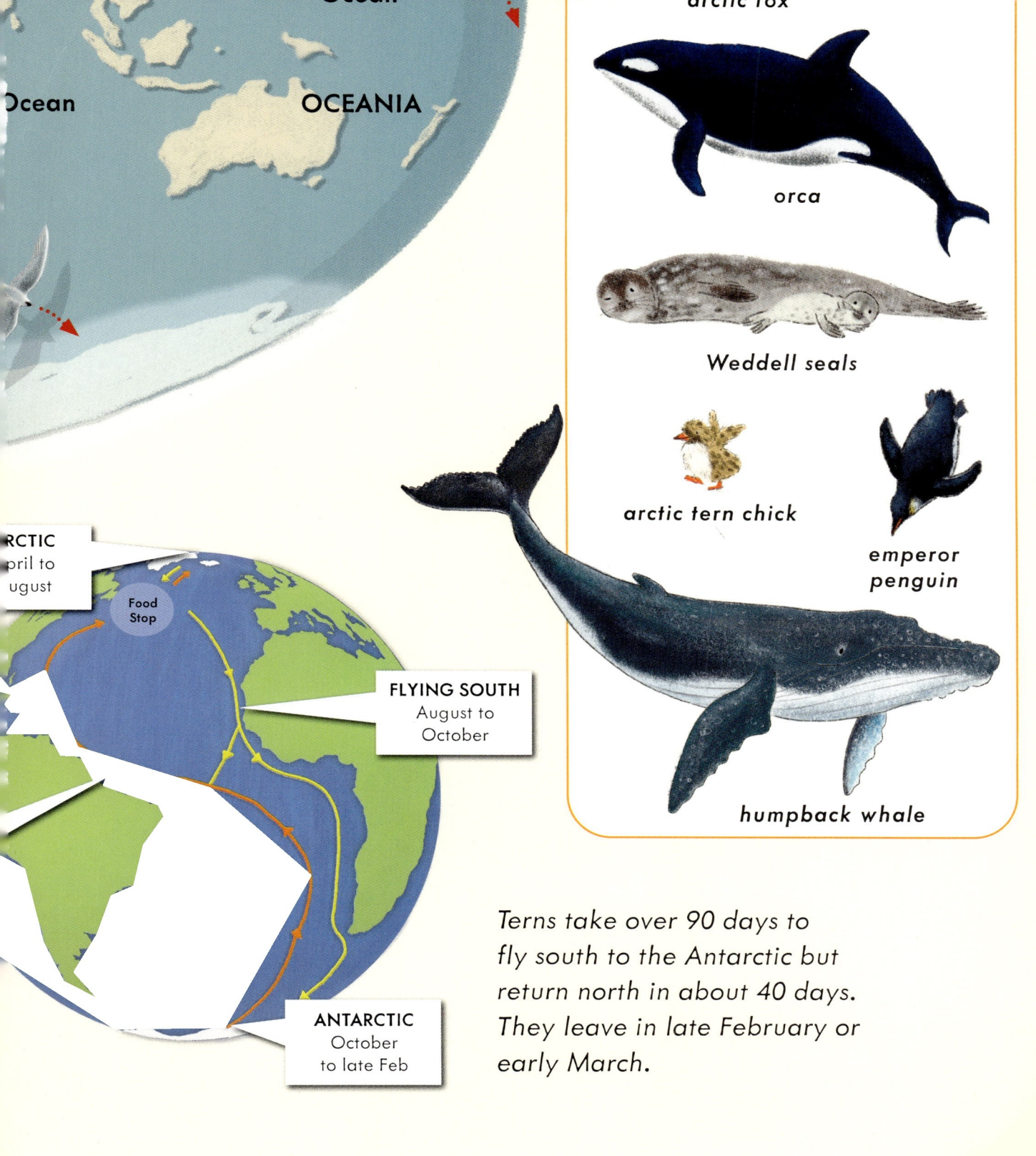

arctic fox

orca

Weddell seals

arctic tern chick

emperor penguin

humpback whale

FLYING SOUTH
August to October

ANTARCTIC
October to late Feb

Terns take over 90 days to fly south to the Antarctic but return north in about 40 days. They leave in late February or early March.

**Look, I have found a mate.
It is time to build a nest.**

The tern is fully grown when she is three or four years old, with all her adult coloring and feathers. She is ready to have her own chicks.

open